SELF TALKS

WITH

MICHAEL TAVON

&

MOONSOULCHILD

ISBN: 9798663137461

"Healing can get ugly; healing may come with a thousand tears. And that's okay. Embrace that dark side of healing, so you can tap into the light that's been buried deep inside you."

-     Michael Tavon

"With your heart, listen
silence your ego
Be in tune with your intuition
The past you must let go
Learn yourself in new ways,
Stop wasting precious moments
Sulking in pain."

-     Michael Tavon

"Yes, heartbreaks, mistakes, and rejection hurt like hell, but the difference between success and failure is YOUR mindset. Will you dwell in your sadness or will you take the pain and create magic from it?"

-     Michael Tavon

"My spirit was set free
Once I let go of
the burden of wanting
to be understood."

- Michael Tavon

"Watch the friends who celebrate with you when you share good news with them. Those are the friends who truly support you.

Watch the friends who sit in awkward silence when you tell them about your accomplishments. Those are the friends who secretly envy you.

Watch the friends who try to one up you every time you speak proudly of your success. Those are the friends who created a one-sided competition with you."

-      Michael Tavon

"Find the power in your voice,

Discover the strength in your words. Once you find the courage to speak to the universe, your scattered stars will realign into the constellation that will lead to the life you deserve."

- Michael Tavon

"Life is too short to stress about money or the lack thereof. Life is too short to stress over a job that will replace you within 48 hours if you drop dead today. With that said, only today is promised so live abundantly and explore."

-       Michael Tavon

"If your parents tried their best to raise you forgive them for their mistakes. Forgive them for disappointing you. Remember, they're humans who are deeply flawed with traumas they never healed from. Consider their hardships. Consider the pressure that comes with being a parent. They have the tremendous responsibility of working hard while trying to raise a human into being a good person. So, if they tried, forgive them. I'm sure they did everything out of love."

-       Michael Tavon

"No matter how big or small,
all progress is worth celebrating
All growth deserves to be recognized
Any change for the better deserves
An applause
Be proud of this moment."

-       Michael Tavon

"Don't doubt this blessing. You deserve it, so appreciate it before the universe strips it away from you."

- Michael Tavon

"Learning yourself is like an ever-flowing river. You will feel: the lows, the highs, the retrogrades, and forward waves. However, the motion, soak it in, allow the water to douse over your existence, and re-emerge as a new powerful you."

-      Michael Tavon

"While having self-talks please speak to yourself with good intentions. Feed your mind words of encouragement and tell yourself everything will be fine."

-       Michael Tavon

"A lover who supports you
A lover who builds with you
A lover who listens
A lover who doesn't
invalidate your feelings
A lover who embraces your lifestyle
A lover who cares
about your mental and physical health
Once you find that person, you'll discover
What true love is."

-   Michael Tavon

"I'm so proud of you! Look back to see how far you've come, take a deep breath to bask in your greatness. You deserve this. Don't let anyone tell you different."

- Michael Tavon

"While you're 'testing' your friendships by
seeing who will contact you first, you may have
a friend who is spiraling out of control because
you were too self-centered to give them a
shoulder to lean on when they needed you, but
it's not too late. Reach out and put some
sunshine in their raining eyes."

-       Michael Tavon

"The key to my success was surrounding myself
with honest friends, not yes-men. I surrounded
myself with friends who understood my passion
and gave constructive support. Even when it
was something I didn't want to hear. People
who care about you want to see you win and
won't allow you to make a fool of yourself in the
process."

- Michael Tavon

"Complaining too much
is like a slap in God's face
show more gratitude
and watch the universe shower
Blessings down on you
So please be patient,
Your flowers only bloom
when you give them time."

- Michael Tavon

"Your heart has been beaten and bruised that
your heartbeat feels numb these days but
continue to feel your way through life. Your
love is beautiful despite the tragedies your heart
has endured."

- Michael Tavon

" People with good hearts are always the most
tired because we're restless. We possess so much
hope for the broken souls and corrupt world
that it takes a toll on our mental health; when
we witness so much hatred. I pray we never
lose sight of the good. I pray we never lose hope.
I pray that we continue to pursue what's right. I
pray we continue to pursue justice and fight for
love and equality."

-       Michael Tavon

Self-Talk Mantra I

I will have a great day
I will not give negative spirits the power to
break through my shield of positivity
I am in complete control
I will not react to hateful comments
or actions today
I will rise above any pettiness

Self-Talk Mantra II

I messed up,
I will learn from my mistakes
I will become wiser and more conscious
by soaking in this lesson
I will not beat myself up,
I am human,
I am learning
how to become a better me

Self-Talk Mantra III

I may cry
But I am far from weak
I may feel pain
But I am far from broken
I've been disappointed
But I am far from hopeless
I am always searching for clarity
I will never stop feeling

"Life is precious
Spend more time appreciating
Every moment the sun sets on your skin
And the days you share with loved ones.
We all know,
In the blink of an eye
Everything we know and love
Can fade to black"

- Michael Tavon

"You're tired but I will not let you give up. You have so much more to offer. So much more to accomplish, and a whole world to explore. I know it's a lot of pressure to keep going, but remember the old cliché, *Pressure makes diamonds*. So, keep shining my friend."

- Michael Tavon

"Love, we all were born to give and receive it,
but somewhere down the line it became scarce;
something hard to find."

- Michael Tavon

"Say 'I love you' as often as possible. Say it to your friends. Say it to your siblings and parents. Most of all say it to yourself."

- Michael Tavon

"When's the last time you took yourself on a
date?
Or treated yourself to a dinner or movie?
Or spoiled yourself in a spa?
Or took a stroll on the beach?

Some people think it's sad to go out or explore
places without company, but aloneness becomes
wholeness once you become comfortable with
doing things for yourself with yourself."

-        Michael Tavon

"Never question your passion. Don't give the doubters the satisfaction by proving them right."

- Michael Tavon

<u>2020</u>

As confusing, challenging, and uncomfortable
this year has been.
We're still here to unlearn every lie we were
taught. We still have the opportunity to grow
mentally, so we can gain a deeper
understanding of each other. As emotionally
taxing 2020 has been, we are now gaining the
clarity to see why we should love our sisters,
brothers, and others for their differences. Each
moment we are blessed to feel, we become
stronger. In the end 2020 will be the war that
will turn us into the warriors who will fight for
each other and Mother Earth.

"A broken heart is mendable don't

wallow in self-doubt.

Take the broken piece to recreate Something

stronger and richer.

This time make it more exclusive,

less accessible.

 The heart needs to be

given to the people worthy of your space."

-       Michael Tavon

"You're putting in overtime effort to make
things work. The more you pull the more they
push you away. You wish things would go back
to the way they were. Unfortunately, the past is
a flame you can't rekindle. You may not see this
now but redirecting your efforts into your
dreams will be more rewarding than wasting
time on a love that's fizzled out."

-      Michael Tavon

"When life threw her stones

She made a mountain

When life blew storms

her way she created a forest

No matter what obstacles life presents

she finds a way to survive and thrive"

-       Michael Tavon

"She is tired of giving
all her love to part-time lovers.
Constantly wasting time
trying to chase forever
in people who eventually disappear."

-    Michael Tavon

"I will take the time to heal properly
I won't rush into new relationships Because I
hate being alone
I will learn to trust myself
I will learn to love my solitude
I will find the meaning behind my suffering
I will overcome."

- Michael Tavon

Affirmation II

(fill in the blank)

I am love

I am light

I am _____

"The voyage to self-discovery gets turbulent at times. The waves, the motion, the unknown, gets scary. The longer you travel the more challenging it gets, that's what it is all about. Facing your hardships will lead you to the fruitful destination you are struggling to reach."

-   Michael Tavon

"Never lose your sanity over someone who
hurts you without a care."

-      Michael Tavon

"I am in love with my refection
I am infatuated with my soul
I am pleased with my growth
I am thankful for growing old."

\-   Michael Tavon

"It hurts now, but the pain will shape me
into the best version of myself."

-Michael Tavon

"She's emotionally wealthy,
And generous when it comes to giving
to those who need it
Even when people come and go,
taking advantage of her heart
It doesn't stop her
she refuses to become cheap
when it comes to giving
because she doesn't want to shortchange the
people in despair."

-      Michael Tavon

"Sometimes, a compromise is necessary to improve the quality of a relationship, but never compromise so much to the point you become a shell of yourself."

-    Michael Tavon

"Today, will be a win
I owe it to myself
To win."

- Michael Tavon

"Heartbreak is bitch from hell,
but don't let it turn you into a vindictive
person.
Through the pain
You must handle it with grace
Take a step back
Rest
Reset
Heal in plain sight"

- Michael Tavon

"Heal before you search for love again,

using relationships as a coping mechanism

is not healthy, it's self- destructive."

-       Michael Tavon

<u>Affirmation VII:</u>

<u>(Fill in the blank)</u>

I am in the process of,

I am aware of the work it will take
I am ready for the challenge.

Affirmation VIII:

Today, my heart is filled with joy
And I will spread as much love into the
atmosphere as possible.

Affirmation IX:

(Fill in the blank)

I believe I have what it takes to

And I will not allow anything to hold me

back, not even myself.

Prompt #1

Write a note to your first heartbreak thanking
them for the lesson they taught you.

'I am not defined by the error of my past ways;
I am moving forward with what I have learned
so I won't repeat the same habits over and over
again.'

-Michael Tavon

"Being afraid to start over is holding you back from the future that awaits you."

-   Michael Tavon

"Forgive those who disappointed you. Your heartbeat will feel so much lighter once you let go of the burdens you're holding on to."

- Michael Tavon

"Your future self will thank you for having the courage to remove yourself from everything that's holding you back "

-        Michael Tavon

"To whom this may concern:

Your expectation of me is not my responsibility
to live up to."

-    Michael Tavon

"Listen with the intent to learn. Listen with an open heart. So many people are so caught up in their own ego; they refuse to acknowledge their faults and ignore anything that doesn't align with their flawed beliefs. Part of maturing is realizing you are not always right."

- Michael Tavon

"Drinking your problems away may feel comforting in the moment, but once you sober up those problems will be ready to attack you again. Instead of poisoning your body with a toxic substance, find a positive coping mechanism. Something that will not only inspire you to grow, but also help you heal. "

-    Michael Tavon

"If you don't hold someone you love
accountable for their fascist beliefs, then you are
also part of the problem. "

- Michael Tavon

"Normalize looking into the mirror and telling yourself how proud you are for how far you've come."

-    Michael Tavon

"You know what you need to do but you're afraid of what others may think. What they think of you is not your responsibility to live up to. Only you know what it's like to live inside your mind, so never allow thoughts from the outsiders to steer you away from what you aspire to do. "

- Michael Tavon

"Sometimes we fall into the trap of overworking
ourselves to prove something to the world.
Sometimes we fall into the trap of sleepless
nights to show how hard we're working.
Remember this, your mind deserves a break,
your body needs sleep. You won't accomplish
anything with a tired mind and sore body.
Reward yourself with rest."

-       Michael Tavon

"If someone is willing to learn and receptive enough to listen, teach them without being condescending. Feed them the information without belittling them. Remember, there was a time the information was new to you too. Be the light to their dim."

-      Michael Tavon

"Life is too short, explore every interest. Explore every passion."

- Michael Tavon

How many times do you critique yourself a day?

How many times a day do you show appreciation to yourself?

If you realize you give more attention to the former, please change it.

- Michael Tavon

"When life feels like you're stepping in
quicksand, keep trudging through the struggle.
The more effort you put the easier the path will
become. Giving up is not an option."

-    Michael Tavon

"They broke your heart, but they didn't break you. "

- Michael Tavon

"Love finds you when you're ready, it doesn't need to be chased."

-    Michael Tavon

"Social media can be toxic when you consume
so much negativity. Sometimes it's better for
your mental health to detach from the digital
world and focus on your reality. "

-       Michael Tavon

"I am grateful for
every inch I walk
Every breath I take,
And every mistake I've made.,
Because of this
I am whole."

-       Michael Tavon

"Now more than ever we need to listen. We
need to educate ourselves and each other. We
need to be mindful. We need to be willing to
engage in uncomfortable conversations. There's
no more room for ignorant opinions."

-      Michael Tavon

"Take accountability when you fuck up. Own up to your mistakes. You can rationalize all you want if you're wrong it's okay to admit it. Stop being stubborn and learn from it."

- Michael Tavon

"Relationship trauma is real. and if you don't take the time to heal from your past relationships, any relationship you have will fail."

-      Michael Tavon

"A butterfly isn't born with wings.
A garden doesn't bloom overnight
A tree does not sprout in one day
The most beautiful things take time
Growth is a process
Take the time to appreciate
every step you take."

-       Michael Tavon

"No matter how big or small,
all progress is worth celebrating
All growth deserves to be recognized
Any change for the better deserves
An applause
Be proud of this moment."

-       Michael Tavon

"Be in harmony with your soul and listen when
your body speaks to you."

- Michael Tavon

"Whether it's straight, crooked, or gapped, your smile is beautiful, because it has the power to provide warmth and brighten someone's day. Your smile is the sun."

- Michael Tavon

"Practice the art of reacting less. Some people say or do things to gaslight a negative reaction from you. Sometimes silence is more powerful than words. Keep your power by remaining unbothered and blocking them from your life."

- Michael Tavon

"Keep in mind some 'friends' want to see you do well as long as you're not doing better than them."

-    Michael Tavon

Things that bring me peace:

1) Staring at the night sky
2) The sound of rain
3) Affection
4) Hot Tea
5) Burning incense
6) Stretching

'True love does not require a chase. Effort should be reciprocated. Interest should be mutual. You'll feel the difference once you find the one who matches your energy. "

-        Michael Tavon

"How many times have you broken down then built yourself back up? This right here is just the makings of a new beginning. You'll defeat this struggle; tomorrow is waiting for you to claim your wins."

\-   Michael Tavon

"Always be prepared, you never know when an opportunity is around the corner. Your talent may go unnoticed if you're never prepared to showcase it. "

-     Michael Tavon

"When your soul is at peace the energy you
project will naturally illuminate your physical
being. Therefore, the work you put into your
inner self should always outweigh the work you
put into your physical appearance. When you
work on the ladder, you'll be a sad soul in pretty
clothes. Self-love is the art of focusing on your
inner being, first. "

-    Michael Tavon

"When working on your craft becomes more important than having a good time you'll find yourself outgrowing people you thought you'd grow old with."

-     Michael Tavon

"We're unlearning every lie that was taught to us as children and it's the most liberating feeling in the world"

-   Michael Tavon

"Yesterday is gone and today is all you have, so don't let it go to waste by dwelling on what you'll never get back."

- Michael Tavon

"I am not a facade
I am not a mirage
I am masterfully crafted
From the mistakes I've made
And the lessons I've gained
My entire being is beautiful
I am me,
Unapologetically,
Unapologetically me."

- Michael Tavon

"Listen to your trauma when it says you're not ready for a relationship. Listen to your trauma when it tells you it's time to focus on healing before moving on to someone new."

-    Michael Tavon

"Tell your partner your triggers. Set those
boundaries. If they choose to disrespect your
wishes, then they are not the one best for you."

-      Michael Tavon

"I am whole.
I am never alone
I love myself abundantly
My heart is far from empty"

-    Michael Tavon

I am a blessing
Ready to shine my light
I am a miracle
Grateful for every breath
I am a masterpiece
In the works,
In due time
The world will feel my love.

- Michael Tavon

"The best version of myself began to bloom the moment I stopped giving a fuck about what other people thought of me"

- Michael Tavon

Your fears will consume you if you let them.
Don't let your anxious nerves become of you.
Take control of the way you feel and overcome
what's holding you back from your greatest
dreams. Anxiety is one hell of a mindfuck, but
there's always a way to take your power back.

-     Moonsoulchild

Your heart is the scariest place, yet the most sacred part of you. You're in for a wild ride, but worth every moment. You were meant to love who you love, good and bad. They will be a blessing or a lesson, sometimes both.

-       Moonsoulchild

Don't ever give up on love, it's the most genuine feeling in the world, when someone loves you how you deserve. You may encounter many wrong ones who may make you reconsider, but don't let someone who doesn't know how to love, make your heart change.

-     Moonsoulchild

If it's sadness you feel, feel it then leave it
behind. Don't let it consume you. Don't let it
define your every moment in life. We feel many
emotions, none are constant. Don't dwell trying
to analyze them, accept them, feel them, live
your life.

-     Moonsoulchild

Sometimes the pain must sting before you see
the way you're being treated is wrong. The one
error we always make is expecting our love to
save, when the one we love can't be saved.
It's up to them to change.

- Moonsoulchild

Your toxic ways lead me to open my eyes and
see the real I was desperately trying to hide.

-      Moonsoulchild

I'm holding everyone who hurt me accountable
for their toxicity until they can take
accountability for their own behavior. I may
have extended our time. I may have loved more.
I may have created toxicity by staying, but they
could have walked away, but they chose to play
my heart to see how long I'd stay holding on.

-    Moonsoulchild

Take accountability for trying to choose what's no longer written trying to create the love that you wished to feel the whole time. Sometimes we blame the other person for hurting us, but we set up the perfect trap for them to do so. We're blinded by the love we wished to have, to feel, we forget to condition the way we receive love we forget to build the foundation because we desperately want to feel love. We let anyone love us, or try, with any ounce we run with it. Sometimes the story was already written, and we try to overwrite it. Sometimes we forget we're being treated wrong, because we convince ourselves that our love will save it. Love is just an emotion we feel, it's not strong enough to save any connection when it's no longer healthy.

-    Moonsoulchild

Being uncomfortable isn't uneasy if it opens
your eyes to the real around you.

- Moonsoulchild

Be the vibe you crave.
Be the energy you wish to attract.
Be the peace you wish to feel.
Be the you, you so desperately hide.

-       Moonsoulchild

We are all toxic to someone because we forced
love when the chapter was written, when the
book was already closed. Our intentions are
pure, but the person and situation weren't right.
We became toxic by chasing everything we
wished to feel.

-        Moonsoulchild

Cut off that toxic person in your life today.
Let them go. Open your eyes and see if you're
not being respected. The love you're giving is
not being reciprocated isn't worth being treated
wrong. Love isn't enough to stay.

- Moonsoulchild

Keep your intentions pure and your soul at peace. Be the vibe only real ones crave.

- Moonsoulchild

I never faked perfection or loved anyone perfect.
I like mine to come as real as possible. I like to
see the flaws that define the unique soul behind
them. I like mine as humanly as possible.

-    Moonsoulchild

Instead of broadcasting your flaws, take a
moment to appreciate what you love about
youself. Speak positive affirmations to yourself,
about yourself. Practice more self-love. Stop
feeding your mind what you loath, your vision
won't ever change.

-      Moonsoulchild

Do something outside your comfort zone for
once. Do something that sets your soul on fire.
Do something that may scare you but will bring
you closer to happiness. Do something.

-      Moonsoulchild

Love is love.

There's no gender, race, or sexuality that can
interfere with love. Don't let anyone dim your
heart. Love with your heart not your eyes.
Never be ashamed of who you are or who you
love. The world isn't ashamed to spread so
much hate, so don't be afraid to be free.

-     Moonsoulchild

It's crazy when your own friends don't support your happiness. It's selfish to want people to stay the same forever. Be more, let your friends grow, let them find happiness. It's your duty as a friend to always be there, even when what makes them happy isn't for you.

-     Moonsoulchild

Don't ever forget why you're still going.
Don't ever forget how you got to where you are.
Don't ever forget how far you've come.
Don't give up now.
Don't give up ever.

- Moonsoulchild

Note to self,

You've made it further than you once imagined.
You always believed in yourself but at times
were lost. You never let yourself down through
the pain, you always loved. Through the
sadness you always smiled. You are strong. You
are brave. You are incredible.

- Moonsoulchild

If you, someone, or something fills your soul with the exact amount of love, happiness, and peace, you wouldn't think of healing. If you're in need of healing, start questioning your trauma, who's in your life, what's in your life that you need to heal from. Let it go.

-    Moonsoulchild

The healing process starts after you let go and move on from everything you're trying to heal from.

- Moonsoulchild

You can't heal from something you're not ready to walk away from. Please understand this will only bring more pain. It will only force more time to heal. Don't let "love" keep you around trauma. Don't let "love" hold you back from your growth.

-       Moonsoulchild

Don't settle for love.
Love is an emotion, something we feel for
ourselves and each other. It's not to hold you
back from doing what's best for you. You will
love a lot of people in your life, it's not healthy
to hold everyone at the standard
of lasting forever.
Some will always fade away.

-      Moonsoulchild

Healing starts from within you. The trauma you've faced. The burdens you're carrying. The regret that's holding you close. You need to let go of everything that makes you feel like you're not enough. If anyone or anything makes you question your worth, that's a sign.

-    Moonsoulchild

Don't let anyone's mask fool you.
If they aren't treating you right, believe them.

-    Moonsoulchild

There's nothing rawer than your fearless soul
shining so much light. Confidence is beautiful,
we all have it. Sometimes it takes us longer to
discover it. We're blinded by the flaws everyone
placed onto us. We saw the picture everyone
painted, all differently. We saw their version of
us. Your perception of me isn't based on how
you hear me, how you see me, or who you
believe I am. Everyone's perception of me will
change. I will outgrow some. Some of the same
who spoke words of love will also speak words
of pain. A lot of the time people love you for
convenience. Some will walk out your life once
they no longer understand who you're
becoming. Don't be afraid, lose all fear when it
comes to loving you. You deserve every ounce
of that love. You deserve to love yourself the
way you love everyone else.

-      Moonsoulchild

Be you, unapologetically.
That's what makes you the most beautiful.

-      Moonsoulchild

If you push me away, you won't find yourself
back in my life. I gave too many chances, too
many times. I don't have it in me anymore, to
fight, to keep rebuilding bridges that already
burnt down.

-   Moonsoulchild

Be a good person.
Be a kind soul.
Be the one who radiates positive energy,
Be the best you can be, but remember,
Don't try reaching perfection,
You're human.

- Moonsoulchild

Open yourself to love again, but don't give your heart away to everyone so easily. You love a lot of souls, but not everyone deserves your heart. Trust your intuition, if it doesn't feel right, leave it.

-     Moonsoulchild

I shut people out too many times.
I took people back too many times.
I gave more than I received, too many times.
I've been misused, misunderstood, and
mistreated. I've been hurt, lost, and ghosted. I
learned too many lessons, myself was the
hardest one.

- Moonsoulchild

Many will be present in your life when they were meant to, doesn't mean their place will forever remain. People grow, don't hold their growth against them, it's inevitable.

- Moonsoulchild

You're scared to love again because you're afraid to get hurt. You're scared to open yourself to someone new without old patterns repeating. It's important to love yourself a little more, so you won't settle for less than you're worth.

-    Moonsoulchild

If you have a big heart, you're someone with a lot of love to give. You gave your heart to many who didn't deserve it, leaving those pieces behind. You tried to save and create versions of love you wanted to exist. You were never dishonest; you were just using love all wrong.

-       Moonsoulchild

I realized I couldn't be upset over holding someone to a higher standard when they never showed they were worthy. I expected more, the many chances I gave. I tried to create this ideal love, friendship, and connection. I overlooked the signs that were written out for me. I didn't take accountability for the times I treated myself less just to be loved more by someone who couldn't love me halfheartedly. I never held anyone accountable for the times they hurt me when I kept taking them back, letting them get close when I should have left them in the dark. A lot of lost connections due to lack of support. Love was there but never strong enough to create an unbreakable bond. I had to work overtime to keep it up. I believed opposites attract, so I spent a lot of time trying to believe our differences we'd conquer, except they were just that, differences. I should have opened my eyes and saw everything clear as presented to me, but I saw with a different vision then, than I do now. I had to learn to be patient with myself and the real before it could ever get presented to me.

-    Moonsoulchild

Normalize loving yourself so freely and
fearlessly, the same way you gave your heart to
everyone who never deserved it.

-   Moonsoulchild

Normalize taking accountability and holding
everyone accountable for who they show up to
be. Don't try rewriting their character because
you saw good in them. We all have good in us,
some of us just weren't made to fit together.

-       Moonsoulchild

Normalize not always being a savior.
Normalize being human.

- Moonsoulchild

One of the hardest things I had to learn was patience, to stop expecting everyone to have the same mindset as I do. To not hold everyone at a higher standard like I hold myself to.

- Moonsoulchild

My mindset differs from a lot of people I've
been close to, my free spirit, I guess you can say
tainted some. They always swore it "Wasn't me"
that I was trying to be someone I wasn't. Not
once did they think, maybe it was them who
couldn't accept me for everything I am.

-    Moonsoulchild

I used to be shy and afraid,
I'm not anymore,
So why not embrace being free.

-     Moonsoulchild

Take a breath.
Release the negative.
Speak the positive into existence.
Tell your loved ones you love them.
Look in the mirror,
Be proud of the person you're becoming.
If you're unable to identify,
Repeat these steps until you do.

-     Moonsoulchild

Life may get overwhelming. You tend to feel, sometimes too much, as you adapt to the healing of your loved ones. Having a good heart can drain you. It's best to take a day for yourself, check in on your own mental health. It's not selfish to take care of you too.

-      Moonsoulchild

Before you rest tonight, say one thing you're
thankful for, pray on it. Pray for better days.
Pray for the hate to fade away. Pray for your
loved ones. Pray for continued love and
happiness. Pray for you, just pray.

-      Moonsoulchild

Social media can be a very dark place. A platform that can be used for such good, such positive. Instead, it's used for so much hate. When you speak how you feel, it gets taken out of context. When speaking for yourself; it gets taken out of context. Nothing you do is good enough.

- Moonsoulchild

There's a lot more trauma in healing than positive. So, before you approach me with something and expect me to agree with you because "I'm a healer" realize, I didn't become whole giving my heart to everyone I loved, it was all the heartache that led me here.

- Moonsoulchild

The problem with most people is they feel
entitled to everything they want. They believe
they deserve to control everything, that they're
always right. Until life knocks them down,
seeing the reality, the only entitlement they have
is to themselves.

-      Moonsoulchild

The problem is you expect too much from
everyone when you can't get it right yourself,
because you're too busy worrying about
everyone else.

- Moonsoulchild

I take accountability for all the souls I hurt because I was selfishly searching to be loved. I didn't give them what they deserved. I take accountability for the wrongs I chose to forget and never rewrite. I take accountability for overlooking my worth trying to be needed.

-      Moonsoulchild

Stop returning to the past every time you're reminded of someone. Stop wondering "what is" or what could have been. It exited your life for a reason, one you'll probably never know. When fate decides, don't try to analyze. Letting go will benefit you.

- Moonsoulchild

Find wholeness in your solitude and I promise
you won't attach loneliness to weakness ever
again.

-      Moonsoulchild

Spend time in your own solitude and learn you.
Stop spending time trying to understand
everyone around you, take time to understand
you. No one can deeply appreciate your
existence if you can't. know your worth, it will
go a long way in every connection you make.

-   Moonsoulchild

I left behind old flames before they burnt me.

-       Moonsoulchild

Don't let anyone trick your kindness for
weakness. Don't let them walk in and out as
they please. They don't deserve open
availability to your heart. they aren't worthy of
your love.

-      Moonsoulchild

Be kind to yourself.
Stop putting so much pressure on yourself when
it comes to anything out of your control. Don't
let yourself fall into hating yourself over
something that wasn't your intention. Don't let
your heart turn cold because of them.

- Moonsoulchild

Hold your loved ones close,
Don't ever make them question your love.

- Moonsoulchild

Letting go of anyone that gets in the way of loving yourself completely. If they genuinely love you, they wouldn't make you choose.

-       Moonsoulchild

I pray you don't lose yourself within hopeless love. I pray you don't let someone reciprocate half their love. I pray you find love that doesn't blind you into believing you're not enough, I pray you see who you are.

-    Moonsoulchild

Stop settling.
Stop trying to find your worth within people
who don't even know theirs.

- Moonsoulchild

You're deserving of the same love you have to give, don't let anyone manipulate you into believing you only deserve to be loved in half.

- Moonsoulchild

Someone will walk into your life and open your soul, a place not many visited. Someone who's patient with you, who takes the time to learn you. Someone who brings peace, never chaos. Do good by them, but don't overdo their stay. If they're meant to go, close the door behind them.

-       Moonsoulchild

Self-love,

A never-ending battle of trying to keep this vision of yourself every time your worth us tested. It's keeping your sanity in check. It's not losing yourself within people while loving them.

- Moonsoulchild

Your love is rare in this world.
Your heart is a precious gift,
Don't let anyone take that from you.

- Moonsoulchild

Fearing love will only bring you further away from it. Love doesn't bring pain, overusing your heart when it has reached its limit will bring pain. You can't make someone love you, you can't make them stay. Never stop loving. Stop giving your heart to people who aren't worthy of it.

- Moonsoulchild

I'm happy knowing I'm not searching for love or acceptance from anyone. I've found peace within another soul after I made peace with myself. I conditioned the love for who comes into my life. I'm happy. No more voids to fill. No more temporary people.

-    Moonsoulchild

You'll never catch me going back to an ex, I
learned from my past. I taught myself if the
bridges burnt, not to rebuild them. We had a
moment in time but forever wasn't written
between us. I taught myself, when the storylines
come to an end, close the chapter, don't fight for
it.

-      Moonsoulchild

Educate yourself on things you don't
understand, knowledge will take you far.
Knowledge is power.

- Moonsoulchild

It's important not to get lost in your heart, as you drown in the love you have for someone else.

-       Moonsoulchild

Learning to let go of someone who you grew to love but didn't love you back breaks your heart. So, you take them back to prove to yourself the pain wasn't for anything. You think it may have not been your time, but don't let history repeat and you lose yourself.

-    Moonsoulchild

Don't stay somewhere you find comfort because
you're too afraid you'll find something that
awakens your soul but may hurt someone else.
Always do right by yourself, when it comes
down to choosing, the universe does the rest.

-      Moonsoulchild

A level of understanding not many can
comprehend, just because someone wasn't good
to you, or couldn't love you the way you loved
them, doesn't mean their heart isn't there. Their
heart isn't close to the way your heart beats.

-       Moonsoulchild

Be kind.
Spread love.
Refrain from feeding into negativity.
Block anything that doesn't bring blessings.
We need more real love in the world,
We have enough hate.

- Moonsoulchild

It's not selfish to love yourself more. It's not selfish to choose you, if you're ever faced with that decision.

- Moonsoulchild

One of the worst things I put myself through,
was trying to fit into a crowd when I already
outgrew the environment.

-       Moonsoulchild

Someone out there is praying to find happiness, love, and peace. Someone out there is speaking the same prayer as you. Hang in there, that someone will make their way to you. Keep praying. Keep loving. Keep the faith.

-    Moonsoulchild

Don't try rebuilding old bridges that burnt down, it won't fit the way it once did. It may take years to rebuild the foundation. You'll never feel the same you once did, you'll always be reminded of that fire that took you both out. Build new bridges that lead to new beginnings.

-       Moonsoulchild

To start the healing process, you must release yourself from what's keeping you from your growth.

- Moonsoulchild

To break free into a butterfly, you need to accept what you can't change and detach yourself from the past. You'll never grow going back to what held you back from your growth.

-    Moonsoulchild

Don't try fitting into an environment you can't
grow within.

-    Moonsoulchild

It's hard being an empath in 2020.

-     Moonsoulchild

You don't need to abandon your heart and turn cold. You need to treat your heart like the precious gift it is and stop giving your love to everyone so easily.

- Moonsoulchild

My actions show my character.
How I react shows my character.
What I say shows my character.

How you see me
How you interpret me
How you make me look,
Doesn't show my character,

It shows yours.

- Moonsoulchild

It's important to never lose yourself throughout
all the versions of you that exist to everyone
else. How they see you isn't your problem. How
they hear you isn't your problem. Many times,
we're a convenience. Many times, we're clouded
by judgment because our mindsets differ.

-   Moonsoulchild

It took me a while to understand I thought outside the norm. my mindset was unmatched, and when it was, it was rare. Battling my own identity growing up was normal, trying to understand I didn't fit in, nor did I stand out, I was a free spirit. I didn't have a crowd I fit into, I blended perfectly in and perfectly out. I take pride in being different, I once feared it. I feared being misunderstood. It was incredibly hard to be loved, to be felt. My love was too intense for some. I was too sensitive, vulnerable, and amiable. I felt too much of everyone, I loved intuitively. Insanely bittersweet to be an empath. I never saw it as feeling too much because being open with my emotions how I'm able to process them. I'm a sucker for feeling, I would never want to numb that. I would never want to be cold, I have too much heart, too much soul to give. I don't blame my heart for the souls it never kept. I don't hold myself at regret for not being kept. I hold myself accountable for all my mistakes but never my flaws. I taught myself to always fight for what's love, what's right, never what I blinded myself

to believe. I witnessed the dishonesty, unhealed,
and unhealthy love. It taught my heart to never
love the way I was loved but to love more,
always. It gave me that authentic, unique, and
that "feel at home" spark. They're the reason I
understand myself more. They taught me the
lesson I needed most now in life. Some are still
teaching me or forever embedded in my soul's
life. Some never met my spirit. Some feared it.
Some will never know it. I've battled for years
trying to accept who I am doesn't need to be
understood, I'm a free spirit. I'm okay with
knowing some will judge but never feel me. I'm
not for the weak nor am I for the healing, I'm the
aftermath of what it's like loving yourself after
the disaster. I'm for the whole, the inspirational.
For those being so hard on yourself, take some
time to love you more without letting
judgements clouded. Love you, no outside
noise. I promise you, only blessings will appear,
only real love will be so.

-      Moonsoulchild

I genuinely fell for someone when I wasn't
searching for love, I was searching for peace. I
was searching for myself and found a friend
who became the love of my life. Sometimes you
need to focus on growing yourself and you'll
run into what's destined for you.

-    Moonsoulchild

Don't let anyone make you feel like where
you're at is wrong because your peace doesn't
involve them. Don't let anyone take you back to
that dark place they once had you before you
sacrificed them for your peace.

-       Moonsoulchild

You're rare,
Open your eyes and stop settling for mediocre.

- Moonsoulchild

Some people don't deserve to know the love
after your growth, close the book.

-       Moonsoulchild

If it disturbs your peace, if it doesn't align with
your growth, it's probably best to keep the door
closed. Don't reopen old wounds. Do what's
best for you.

-     Moonsoulchild

Dear reader,

If you enjoyed the contents of this collection, please help spread the word by

1) Posting about the book via social media and tag our accounts.
Twitter:
@Moonssoulchild & @MichaelTavon

Instagram
@BymichaelTavon and @Moonsoulchild

2) Leave a review on amazon or goodreads
3) Share the book with friends

Any of theses actions would be greatly appreciated and helps tremendously with growing our readership. Thank you for reading,

With love,

Michael and Moon

Made in the USA
Las Vegas, NV
06 November 2021

33869492R00111